my baby's journal

a letter to you

our family tree

our family tree

a baby is an inestimable blessing.

mark twain (1835–1910)

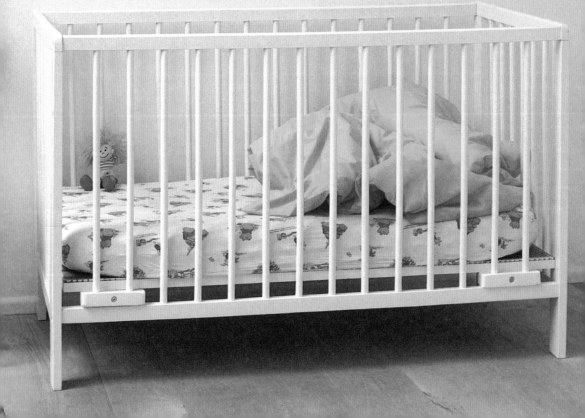

good news

how we felt when we knew you were on the way

your due date

you arrived on

waiting for you

waiting for you

mommy's feelings

_____
_____
_____
_____
_____
_____

daddy's feelings

_____
_____
_____
_____
_____
_____

we first heard your heartbeat

_____
_____

mommy first felt you move

_____
_____

we first saw you on the ultrasound scan

_____
_____

getting ready

getting ready

buying your layette

childbirth and parenting classes

decorating the nursery

decorating the nursery

the colors we chose

the paper and paint we chose

the fabric we chose

the crib, armoire, and changing table we chose

the finishing touches

the baby shower

the baby shower

given by

where and when

the guests

the gifts

girls' names

our favorite girls' names

_____
_____
_____
_____
_____
_____
_____
_____
_____

why we like them

_____
_____
_____
_____
_____
_____
_____
_____

girls' names

our final choice

your baby names and nicknames

boys' names

our favorite boys' names

why we like them

boys' names

our final choice

_____

_____

_____

_____

_____

_____

your baby names and nicknames

_____

_____

_____

_____

_____

_____

life began with waking up and loving my mother's face.

george eliot (1819–1880)

your birth

the time

the place

your weight

your length

your hair was

your eyes were

who was present

your birth

mommy's story

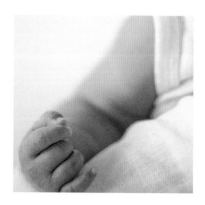

your birth

daddy's story

your first photo here

hospital identity tag here

cards and gifts

cards, gifts, and flowers received

_____

_____

_____

_____

_____

_____

_____

_____

_____

_____

_____

_____

_____

_____

_____

_____

_____

_____

_____

your very first visitors

your very first visitors

their messages to you

your birth announcement card

birth announcement card here

your footprint

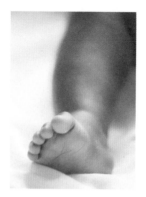

baby's footprint here

your handprint

baby's handprint here

a babe in a house is a well-spring of pleasure.

martin farquar tupper (1810–1889)

coming home

our address

_____

_____

_____

photo of our home here

your first night at home

your first night at home

where you slept

_____

you fell asleep at

_____

you woke up at

_____

you fell asleep again at

_____

you woke up again at

_____

you fell asleep again at

_____

you woke up again at

_____

your first visitors at home

your first visitors at home

your first visitors

they thought you looked like

settling down

settling down

your hungry times

your wakeful times

your sleepy times

you cry when

you like it when

bathtime

bathtime

your first bath

how you reacted

your favorite bath toys

your favorite bathtime games

bedtime

bedtime

you first slept in your own room

you first slept through the night

your favorite lullabies

your favorite bedtime toys

your bedtime routine

bye baby bunting
daddy's gone a-hunting
gone to get a rabbit skin
to wrap the baby bunting in

traditional nursery rhyme

you first focused your eyes

you first followed an object with your eyes

you first lifted your head

you first grasped and held an object

you first found your hands

you first found your feet

you first sucked your thumb or a pacifier

you first smiled

you first cooed

you first laughed

you first said "mama"

you first said "dada"

you first rolled right over

you first sat up alone

you first crawled on your tummy

you first crawled on your knees

you first pointed

you first grasped with your finger and thumb

you first clapped your hands

you first waved goodbye

you first pulled yourself up to stand

you first stood unaided

you first walked unaided

you first walked outside

you first fed yourself

you first had your hair cut

we bought your first pair of shoes

you first kissed mommy and daddy

weight and height

weight and height

birth

1 month

2 months

3 months

4 months

5 months

6 months

7 months

8 months

9 months

10 months

11 months

12 months

your first teeth

your first teeth

first tooth
_____

second tooth
_____

third tooth
_____

fourth tooth
_____

fifth tooth
_____

sixth tooth
_____

seventh tooth
_____

eighth tooth
_____

ninth tooth
_____

tenth tooth
_____

_____

_____

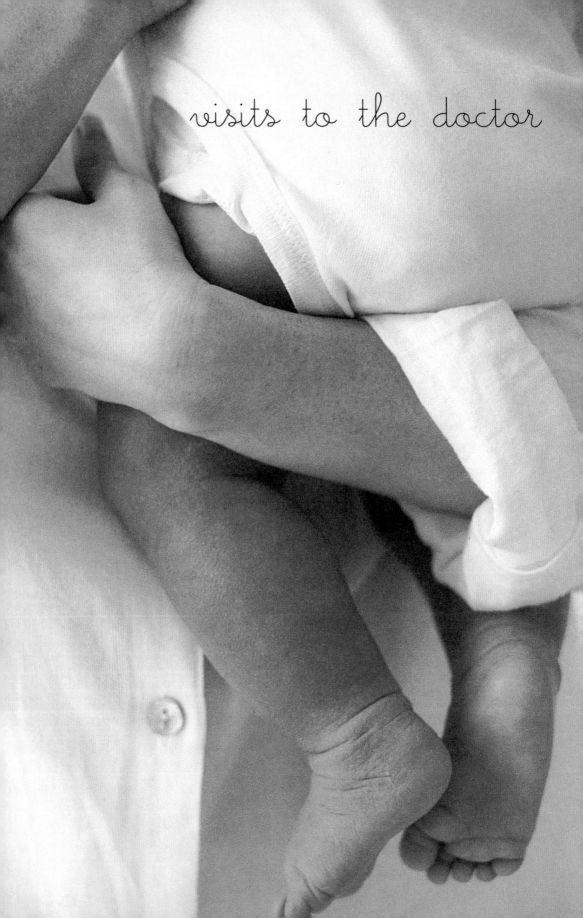

visits to the doctor

visits to the doctor

the name of our doctor

immunizations

allergies

illnesses

'I have no name:
I am but two days old'
what shall I call thee?
'I happy am
joy is my name'
sweet joy befall thee!

william blake (1757-1827)

your first foods

your first solids

_____

_____

_____

_____

_____

how you reacted

_____

_____

_____

_____

_____

your first finger foods

_____

_____

_____

_____

_____

mealtime milestones

you first sat in a highchair

you first used your fingers

mealtime milestones

you first used your spoon

you first drank from a cup

your food likes and dislikes

foods you love

_____
_____
_____
_____
_____
_____
_____
_____
_____

foods you hate

_____
_____
_____
_____
_____
_____
_____
_____
_____

mealtime rituals

your highchair

your favorite bowl and spoon

fun and games at mealtimes

your favorite recipes

your favorite recipes

the sweetest flowers in all the world,
a baby's hands.

charles algernon swinburne (1837–1909)

first outings

your first outing in your stroller

your first trip to the park

your first trip in a car

your first trip on a train

your first trip on a bus

your first trip on a plane

your first outings

to see your grandparents or other family members

your first outings

to see our friends

your first vacation

your first vacation

where we went

when we went

how we got there

where we stayed

your first vacation

what we did

_____
_____
_____
_____
_____
_____
_____

new friends we made

_____
_____
_____
_____
_____
_____
_____

your first vacation

our favorite memories

mother's arms are made of tenderness, and sweet sleep blesses the child who lies therein.

victor hugo (1802–1885)

celebrations

magical moments during your first year

your first christmas

your first christmas

where we celebrated

who celebrated with us

the gifts you received

what you wore

your first birthday

your first birthday

how we celebrated

who celebrated with us

what we ate

what you wore

your naming day

your naming day

how we celebrated

_____

_____

_____

who celebrated with us

_____

_____

_____

_____

_____

_____

_____

_____

_____

how you behaved

_____

_____

_____

what you wore

_____

_____

_____

where did you come from, baby dear?
out of the everywhere into here.

george macdonald (1824-1905)

your favorite...

books

tv shows and videos

songs and lullabies

nursery rhymes

fairy tales

toys

soft toys

clothes

_____

_____

_____

_____

_____

_____

_____

_____

accessories

_____

_____

_____

_____

_____

_____

_____

_____

people

places

little friends

games

playgroups and activities

acknowledgments

cover photography by polly wreford.
all other photography by debi treloar, except for photographs of
imani and harry by lena ikse-bergman.

with many thanks to our adorable little models: amber, antonia,
bruno, darcey, erin, florence, harry, imani, jessica, max, tobey
and sorcha. thanks also to their parents.

all wooden toys courtesy of oggetti,
135 & 143 fulham road, london sw3 6rt

First published in the UK in 2002.
This edition published in the UK in 2008 by
Ryland Peters & Small
20–21 Jockey's Fields
London WC1R 4BW

Published in the US in 2008 by
Ryland Peters & Small, Inc
519 Broadway
5th Floor
New York, NY 10012

RYLAND

PETERS

& SMALL

LONDON NEW YORK

10 9 8 7 6 5 4 3 2   (PINK JOURNAL)
10 9 8 7 6 5 4 3 2   (BLUE JOURNAL)
30 29 28 27 26 25 24 23 22   (YELLOW JOURNAL)

ISBN 978-1-84597-717-7 (PINK JOURNAL)
ISBN 978-1-84597-716-0 (BLUE JOURNAL)
ISBN 978-1-84172-292-4 (YELLOW JOURNAL)

Printed in China